FALLEN, FALLIN!
IN LOVE; THIS 'FALL'

ABHIJEET PADHY

XpressPublishing
An imprint of Notion Press

No.8, 3rd Cross Street,CIT Colony,
Mylapore, Chennai, Tamil Nadu-600004

Copyright © Abhijeet Padhy
All Rights Reserved.

ISBN 978-1-64661-720-3

This book has been published with all efforts taken to make the material error-free after the consent of the author. However, the author and the publisher do not assume and hereby disclaim any liability to any party for any loss, damage, or disruption caused by errors or omissions, whether such errors or omissions result from negligence, accident, or any other cause.

While every effort has been made to avoid any mistake or omission, this publication is being sold on the condition and understanding that neither the author nor the publishers or printers would be liable in any manner to any person by reason of any mistake or omission in this publication or for any action taken or omitted to be taken or advice rendered or accepted on the basis of this work. For any defect in printing or binding the publishers will be liable only to replace the defective copy by another copy of this work then available.

This book is dedicated to my Dad Nilamani Padhy & Mom Sanjukta Padhy. My beautiful sisters & my insane buddies. This book is the product of your love & belief in me.

Contents

Acknowledgements — *vii*

❣Confessions Of A Secret Admirer❣

1. The Love That Accrues Forever — 3
2. The Soothing Rain — 5
3. Let's Celebrate Life — 7

❣High School SweetHearts❣

4. "us" — 11
5. Broken Angel's — 13
6. Prom Night — 15

❣Masterpiece❣

7. Holocausts Of Time — 19
8. The 'missing' Piece — 21

❣One Kiss Less❣

9. Melody Drug — 25
10. Those Luscious Lips — 27
11. Fallen! Falling — 28

❣Fool's Paradise❣

12. 'oops' — 33
13. Frozen — 34

❣The Binding Envelope❣

14. What If It's Not True? — 39
15. 21st July — 41
16. Wink! — 43
17. Binding Envelope — 45

Acknowledgements

It's a glorious day as I sit down to pen these thanks, the dog napping on my shoe, the cat smiling at me & the love birds singing from the top of the Peepal bush. Ok! *Dad & Mom*, without your love & values, I'm incomplete & believe me, 'I love you more than just 3000'. Thanks a million to you *Manish & Mansoor* for your regular taunts, ever helpful sarcasm's & for reviewing my works, even if it was in the middle of midnight. Now if you think I am crazy? You should meet my sister's! I'm much obliged to my sister's *Rashmi, Susmi, Tapaswini, Sampu, Kallu, Sibangi, Ani & Kavya* thanks for your constant support & madness. A loud shout out to my crazy & insane friends *Soumya, Pinkismita, Divya, Biswa, Amar, Sanjeeb, Sanket, Sarba, Saila, Jeebananda, Chandu, Sus & Subho* for hanging onto me when I went batshit crazy. My teachers *Sakshi Singh & Bhagyalaxmi* ma'am for tolerating all kinds of stuff in class, yet supporting me to write more, you are & forever will be the 'best teachers' of my life. Finally, thanks to Lord for giving me the love of my life, I'm planning to tongue kiss her, oh! Wait, I might already have.

❣Confessions of a secret Admirer❣

"It's simple, sweet but not sober, it has no conditions it's for free, try it sometime; maybe then you wanna fall in love with me.
"

1. The love that accrues forever

(I remember having a crush on my childhood bestie but not having enough courage to speak to her, it was my college reunion & I finally got a chance, in front of everyone to confess my love; to confess & say her....)

My love for you accrues forever,
it's pristine, it's pure;
it doesn't want you in my arms,
neither it wants you to kiss.

It wants to see you smile,
it wants to make you laugh,
it wants to help you when you're done,
and then be with you;
when you have none.

My love is old, but not futile,
I am yours but you don't have to be mine,
there's a fine line between love and lust,
which I don't want to cross,
because sometimes in love,
everything that you have; is lost.

Still, my love for you accrues forever,
it's simple, sweet but not sober,
it has no conditions it's for free,
try it sometime;
maybe then you wanna fall in love with me.
(But, wait! my feelings were already confessed, by somebody else..... crushing my dreams to ashes.)

2. The Soothing Rain

(But life's tough, she secretly said to him 'yes' that day in college reunion and they hid it from everyone, literally everyone; until she told me how that guy cheated on her after all these years. She was inconsolable, gutted & heart broken. She laid her head on my shoulders & thats when it started to rain; easing our pain.)

It rains and it rains,
it takes all my pain,
I am relived;
I feel rejuvenated;
when it rains & it rains.

These are not drops, which merely fall on the ground,
they pass through my heart;
and cross my mind,
few which touched my lips & rejuvenated my veins,
when it rains & it rains.

It rains hard,
but I don't need a shed to hide,
I am done with wind hitting me,
with fog surrounding my eyes,
when it rains & it rains.

FALLEN, FALLIN!

It's beautiful;
it's mesmerizing;
it pokes sun to create a rainbow,
& the next moment teases rainbow to form a sunshine.
when it rains & it rains.

It rains & it rains,
the sky pours its heart out,
the cloud interpolates new dreams,
with each passing droplet;
human's life change,
when it rains & it rains.
(My life too changed, I confessed her ...)

3. Let's celebrate life

(The rain had washed away all our pain & we both fell in love little by little, drop by drop. But there was one final confession left, It was not that I was afraid to confess 'Him' but you know, when you date your 'best friend's' little sis; life's gotta be uneasy)

Let's celebrate life,
with little insults,
little bit of joy,
by having each other's company,
till I speak & you annoy.

You can ask me,
but I won't answer,
what you seek,
is not far either,
but those little joys of watching you,
scratch your head; Ah! that view is far better.

'The better the bitter,
the bitter the bite',
truths that you hid from me,
by accepting all my lies,
you became my tiniest family,
a family which enjoys my lies.

You were my father in need,
my mother with love,
my brother in arms,
you were my enemy at times,
but, while solving your troubles,
I found a friend for life.

We have become what we always wanted,
so let's celebrate life,
let me trouble you a little more,
'by asking your sister to be my wife',
& I remember 'Him' beating the shit out of me,
& beating again for hiding from him; my love life.

He scratched his head,
this time with questions infinite;
I recalled, 'The better the bitter,
the bitter the bite',
& he completed, 'promise me, you'll keep her happy,
or else you will be the one to demise'.
(And we burst into laughs with a big Irish wine & I kept dating his sister till she became my wife.)

❣High School SweetHearts❣

"What's so magical? ; "Us" you replied, Keeping a hand on my lips."

4. "Us"

(Something special happens at high school, friends become your life, the canteen becomes your lifeline and amid these, there is a girl whom you remember a lifetime.)

What's so whimsical about you?
the fantasy of your love,
or is it the simplicity of your soul.

You push me to the edge of life,
and pull me;
just before I fall for you.

You stop me from holding you,
in my thoughts,
but wildly kiss me before I leave.

What's so magical?
"Us" you replied,
keeping a hand on my lips.

Your incomplete short answers,
still hovers around my question,
keeping me guessed, always.

Perhaps that's what is whimsical,
magical; between "us",
the high school sweethearts.

5. Broken Angel's

(They broke up after high school as they thought their goals and careers were different, but somehow both landed in the same college, although in different streams.)

Some days back in the time,
you said you were mine,
I wish today; we were together.

Now that I see,
you with my friend,
making out; I shatter.

'High school sweethearts',
as they use to call us,
do you still remember?

Do you feel,
hearts pumping, blood rushing,
when we see each other.

(And then a group of colleagues saw us staring at each other and asked.....)
'Hey! High school sweethearts',
are you looking for love again?

do you wish to be together?

Do you feel,
like forgiving, start dreaming,
& be sweethearts forever.

6. Prom Night

(A year passed, they were invited to the high school prom and once they met, their heart throbbed, hands shivered but only eyes talked in eerie silence.)
(He said)
We had parted ways,
in many ways;
but we felt alone.

(She said)
What did I do?
why didn't you;
take the step to be true.

(He said)
You should have told be,
be a little bold to me;
when I was wrong?

(She said)
You should have slapped me,
you should have kissed me,
but never let me go alone.

(He said)
So come back to me,
we are not meant to be,
home alone.

From high school to college,
so sweet was your knowledge,
I couldn't have passed alone.

(She said)
So in the test of my life,
be the 'best' of my life,
I can't imagine my life with someone else.

(She hugged him and the differences resolved, the prom night turned out to be their night. They danced, kissed & sang tunes of life.)
Perhaps that's what is whimsical,
Magical; between "us",
The high school sweethearts.

❣Masterpiece❣

*"You're the final piece, To my hearts struggle,
Complete me; Make me your masterpiece."*

7. Holocausts of time

(She was there lying lifeless like a body without a soul, wanting to go away to meet them who left her. But, not without one last dying wish.)

The holocausts of my broken heart,
are spread across the time,
will you find it for me?
before I die.

One is with my family,
my dad's smile;
my mom's home cooked food,
and my sisters love.
(The picture of her family)

One is with my friend,
who survived my bad jokes,
entertained all my life,
& held me tight in my bad times.
(Her friends Diary)

The last one is with whom,
I promised to cross the seven seas of life,
the final piece of solace,

the final piece to my puzzled life.

(His son was right along with her all this time, finally completing her wishes by bringing her family(photo) and friends(old memories) together, just before she breathed her final breath.)

8. The 'Missing' piece

(In the quest of the final missing piece, he walked to his father's grave and read her final message)

A missing piece of peace,
If you can find for me,
I could be;
Your masterpiece.

Little by little; with happiness,
If you can fill me,
I would be;
Your solace.

In my dark times,
If you can light me,
I would be;
Your fortune.

I will be everything,
You choose me to be,
Just be mine,
In this lifetime.

You're the final piece,

To my hearts struggle,

Complete me;

Make me your masterpiece.

(And he left the message on the grave of his mother, besides the grave of his father; completing each other's wish to be finally together, as 'the masterpiece'.)

❣One kiss less❣

"But some things never change, for lust was our only access, from this worldly conundrum, although one kiss less!"

9. Melody Drug

Kidding me, with your body,
watching me unfurl,
have you watched 'fury'?
because now; you are going to get 'stormed'.

Caressing me with your lips,
from head, heart till toe,
where you want to go baby,
wake me, where you want to go.

Trapping me in your eyes,
you have caged my soul,
now, half of me is with me,
half of me with you.

(Then she said with force....)
Then take me to the walls,
let the moans be louder,
let the bed speak our mess,
from each nook & corner.

Let my melody, drug you,
touch you, with my tongue,

FALLEN, FALLIN!

your skin is like soothing music,
let me play your body like a song.

10. Those luscious lips

Just like the water in river,
unsettling with incessant rains,
you flew in my dreams,
making me unconscious with your luscious lips.

Your soft, sultry desires,
have painted me in pink,
you have a mountain to climb,
before you sip a drink.

"Do you feel important, now", I asked gently,
kissing ever so softly, her hand,
she woke up & dressed;
& started leaving my homeland.

I stopped her;
and asked her why?
she kissed my forehead; and left saying,
'love has always made me cry'.

11. Fallen! Falling

Fallen! Falling from atop,
after reaching cloud nine,
it was difficult to stop thinking,
about someone whom I considered mine.

She sounded like heaven,
her body felt so divine,
she smelled like love,
in her luscious smile.

She tasted like forever,
I wanted her to be mine,
& there she was in search of,
another masculine.

It was a cuckoldry,
where lust over took love,
as three days of charm,
had made us crave.

But some things never change,
for lust was our only access,
from this worldly conundrum,

although one kiss less.

❣Fool's Paradise❣

"In a moment of 'oops', I saw many dreams come true, it was no reality, but the words felt so true."

12. 'Oops'

("She looked at me and sighed away, then I looked at her and looked till her eyes met mine and we fell for each other, right away", so beautiful isn't it.)

The feeling that took my breath away,
sent my heart into space,
I wondered about my whereabouts,
only to reach the planet of 'solace'.

In a moment of 'oops',
I saw many dreams come true,
it was no reality,
but the words felt so true.

It would be too easy with you,
Each of my dream would come true,
But then what would my nightmares do,
They would hate me if I go with you.

So I have decided not to leave you,
But I will live with my fears,
So my pain would love me,
And I could still be, in love with you.

13. Frozen

(But the season of spring didn't last long…it rained, flooded their lives with infinite questions to answer.)
Frozen by dead winds,
we were teased by rain,
emptiness roped our hearts,
and crushed our brain.

It was bloody cold,
but we were alive,
maybe our pain was unforgiiving,
but our senses were live.

It was tempting,
To see a fire burning for me; in another heart,
But, I wanted your warmth,
A little shelter in your heart.

The flood inundated our area,
But love was our boat,
We swum across;
To find another place; remote.

It was time to stand again,

to show how we block rain,
as we never feared pain;
its just another heart; we can repair it again.

❣The Binding Envelope❣

"Yes, you were true, both of us stuck together; by destiny, just as two broken pieces; joined by glue."

14. What if it's not true?

(Ten years ago we promised each other something, from the depth of our eternal hearts, but will she turn up was the question?)
'What if it's not true?
I was hoping for you,
what if you don't turn up?
then, what will I do!'

'Do you remember the relevance?
of reticent chaos in my head,
thinking head over heels about you,
& standing in awe before you'.

'Yes, you were true,
both of us stuck together; by destiny,
just as two broken pieces;
joined by glue'.

The same glue that we applied,
to our envelope,
a message we wrote for each other,
and promised to open it after a decade; together.

We hid it beneath our college playground,

beside a big banyan tree;
locked in a mysterious treasure box,
so it can never be found.

But then, we were so young,
played with little toys of love,
& little wisdom we had,
to correct what went wrong.

The glue started segregating,
a cracked head, two broken hearts; started a war,
by not looking at each other,
& going too far.

15. 21st July

Years went by;
it was 2019's, 21st July,
"two days left!"
 a thought of "Will I meet her, a decade later "crossed my mind.

Out of the blue,
I received a request from my college;
the college that I hated the most,
had invited me as their chief alumni.

(Recalling the incident that happened this day, that year)
23rd July, oh! How can I lie?
with one 'samosa' & 'two chai's',
yes, it was my first date,
yet, till date; the best date of my life.

(Back to square one gentlemen!)
But today, as I was nearing my college,
the 'Drip-drop' of rain,
the 'Tick-tock' of clock,
something happened inside.

FALLEN, FALLIN!

I felt elated without reasons,
I smiled like a kid aged nine,
I sang songs of 90's,
just to be reminded by my driver, I am aged twenty nine.

16. Wink!

I was welcomed with garland,
introduced by my dean,
he spoke of my achievements,
my eyes, which cursed him once,
saw a man who wasn't mean.

I addressed the gathering,
occasionally taking a dig at my dean,
recalling the anecdotes of my backbenchers life,
& teaching the new ones,
importance of love, friendship & life.

Then came a woman, rushing;
with a sheet attached, a file in her hand,
the sheet dropped near me;
we both tried to pick it,
we both picked it, held it & felt it.

We picked our tricked eyes;
talking too much at a glance,
"did you lose it! Mr.", She asked,
"what?" I replied, amazed;
"your heart" she said with a wink.

FALLEN, FALLIN!

(The wink which took my heart away)

17. Binding Envelope

(She took the paper and walked away, & I wondered who she was, as she looked like someone close, someone I had known, only to recall a picture still blurred.)

I walked out of the auditorium,
to eat samosa with chai,
but someone pulled me,
those soft hands, that mischievous smile;
"a decade was a long time, don't you think", she smirked.

Yes, it was her,
my pupils dilated,
my heart raced by,
smiles reached my eyes,
"yes, it was!" I replied.

She took me to the college playground,
behind the banyan tree,
"c'mon now start digging" she said,
we dug, sweated & muddled,
 till we finally found 'our box'.

We opened it;
but we didn't find the envelope,

"23rd July 2019, we will be here again,
you will be there either in love or in hate with me,
but we will be together again", he read (dean).

It started raining,
may be the clouds also wanted to cry,
she hugged me, shredding sorrows & pain,
and I, I finally held her in comfort; the rain stopped,
we both grinned, along with the grinning sunshine.

The dean saw all of these,
with moist eyes,
I remember, he once called our parents; for kissing in a closed class,
now he had called them again; to cherish this sight,
'two lover's finally setting things right'.

Then, he accompanied all of us to the 'tapri' outside,
with one 'samosa' & 'two chai's',
yes, it was my 2nd date,
yet, till date; the best date of my life.

(A year later)
A sealed envelope reached his (dean) cabin,
It was an envelope with our marriage card, glued with love forever.

www.ingramcontent.com/pod-product-compliance
Lightning Source LLC
LaVergne TN
LVHW042002060526
838200LV00041B/1839